D1505787

NATURAL WORLD

CROCODILE

HABITATS • LIFE CYCLES • FOOD CHAINS • THREATS

Joyce Pope

RAINTREE
STECK-VAUGHN
PUBLISHERS

A Harcourt Company

Austin   New York
www.steck-vaughn.com

NATURAL WORLD

Chimpanzee • Crocodile • Dolphin • Elephant • Giant Panda
Great White Shark • Grizzly Bear • Hippopotamus
Killer Whale • Lion • Orangutan • Penguin • Polar Bear • Tiger

Cover: An adult Nile crocodile
Title page: A crocodile bares its teeth.
Contents page: A baby crocodile rests on its mother's foot.
Index page: A crocodile on the lookout for its next meal

Published by Raintree Steck-Vaughn Publishers, an imprint of Steck-Vaughn Company

Library of Congress Cataloging-in-Publication Data
Pope, Joyce.
Crocodile / Joyce Pope.
    p.   cm.—(Natural world)
    Includes bibliographical references and index.
    ISBN 0-7398-2764-2 (hard)
    0-7398-3127-5 (soft)
    1. Crocodiles—Juvenile literature.
    [1. Crocodiles.]
    I. Title. II. Series.

Printed in Italy. Bound in the United States.
1 2 3 4 5 6 7 8 9 0 04 03 02 01 00

Picture acknowledgments
Ancient Art & Architecture Collection 37; Ardea 14 (M. Watson), 22 (Ferrero-Labat), 32 (Adrian Warren), 33 (Adrian Warren), 44 middle (M. Watson), 44 bottom (Ferrero-Labat), 45 middle (Adrian Warren); Bruce Coleman Collection 16 (John Visser); Digital Vision 1, 48; Heather Angel 24, 34, 45 top, 45 bottom; FLPA *front cover* (Tony R. Hamblin); NHPA 6 (Rich Kirschner), 8 (Christophe Ratier), 8–9 (Martin Harvey), 10 (Anthony Bannister), 11 (Anthony Bannister), 15 (Anthony Bannister), 20 (Nigel J. Dennis), 26 (Nigel J. Dennis), 28 (Nigel J. Dennis), 35 (John Shaw), 36 (Steve Robinson), 43 (Alberto Nardi), 44 top (Anthony Bannister); Oxford Scientific Films 3 (Mark Deeble and Victoria Stone), 12 (Mark Deeble and Victoria Stone), 13 (Mark Deeble and Victoria Stone), 17 (Mark Deeble and Victoria Stone), 18 (Mark Deeble and Victoria Stone), 19 (Mark Deeble and Victoria Stone), 21 (Mark Deeble and Victoria Stone), 23 (Hilary Pooley), 25 (Frances Furlong), 29 (Mark Deeble and Victoria Stone), 31 (Richard Packwood), 38 (Michael Sewell), 39 (Mark Deeble and Victoria Stone), 40 (Steve Turner), 41 (M. Wendler/Okapia), 42 (Javed Jafferji); Stock Market 27 (Otto Rogge). Map on page 4 by Victoria Webb. All other artwork by Michael Posen.

4790

Contents

Meet the Crocodile

Crocodiles are some of the world's most fearsome reptiles. Most live in rivers and lakes, although some live in coastal waters and in estuaries. This book looks closely at the Nile crocodile, the biggest flesh-eating animal in Africa.

The Nile crocodile spends most of its time in the water, coming out occasionally during the day. In some parts of Africa, the Nile crocodile has been hunted so much that its numbers are dangerously low.

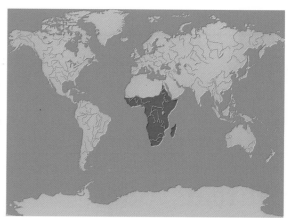

▲ The red shading on this map shows where Nile crocodiles live in Africa. In the distant past, Nile crocodiles swam across the Indian Ocean to the island of Madagascar. There are still a few there today.

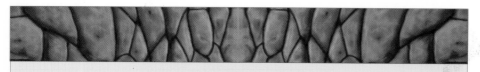

CROCODILE FACTS

The Latin name of the Nile crocodile is *Crocodylus niloticus.*

●

Adult Nile crocodiles sometimes grow larger than 16 ft. (5 m) in length, but most grow to about 11.5 ft. (3.5 m) and weigh about 440 lbs. (200 kg). Males and females look very similar, but males are usually slightly larger.

► An adult Nile crocodile

Legs
The legs sprawl out from the sides of the body when the crocodile is resting. In the water, they are used for steering.

Eyes
The crocodile's eyes are close together on the top of its head. It can lie almost submerged but can still see what is going on above the water's surface. When it swims underwater, it keeps its eyes open. They are protected by transparent eyelids.

Tail
The crocodile moves its tail from side to side to propel itself through the water.

Skin
Crocodiles are protected by heavy skin, with bony scales along the back and tail. The scales are called osteoderms.

Ears
The ears are high on the side of the crocodile's head. They do not have outer ears, like humans. But special flaps of skin protect them from the water.

Feet
The front feet have five toes, and the back feet have four. All have blunt claws. The hind feet are partly webbed.

Jaws
The muscles that close the jaws are very strong, but the muscles that open them are relatively weak.

Nostrils
The crocodile's nostrils are set high at the end of its snout. This way it can breathe when the rest of its body is underwater.

Teeth
The crocodile has more than 60 sharp, pointed teeth. If a tooth gets worn down or broken, it is quickly replaced by another tooth. An adult crocodile about 13 ft. (4 m) long will have already replaced each tooth about 45 times.

▼ The alligator lives by slow-flowing waters in the Carolinas, Florida, and eastern Texas. It is the most studied and best known of all the crocodile's relatives. This picture shows that alligators are dark gray in color. Crocodiles tend to be brown or greenish.

Ancestors and Relatives

Crocodiles are often described as "living fossils," because they have survived almost unchanged since the age of the dinosaurs about 64 million years ago. They are probably more like dinosaurs than any other living creature.

In the past, there were many kinds of crocodiles. Some were huge and preyed on dinosaurs. Others were tiny and fed on mouse-sized mammals.

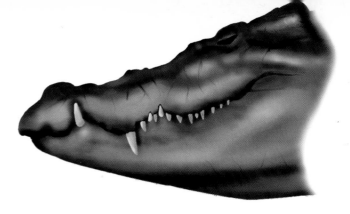

Some ancient crocodiles lived all their lives in the sea. Beautifully preserved fossils show that they had fins on their tails and fed on squid-like creatures.

Today, the Nile crocodile has twenty-one close relatives throughout the world. Thirteen of them are true crocodiles, seven are alligators and caimans, and one is the gavial. The slender-snouted crocodile and the dwarf crocodile also live in Africa.

What's the Difference?

Crocodiles and alligators look alike, but crocodiles generally have shorter and broader jaws. When an alligator or caiman closes its jaws, all its teeth are hidden from view. But a crocodile cannot hide them all. When its mouth is shut, the fourth tooth from the center is visible on each side.

The gavial feeds only on fish. It has very long, narrow jaws with lots of sharp pointed teeth for grabbing and holding its slippery prey.

▲ Even when a crocodile has its mouth shut, it can't help showing some of its sharp pointed teeth. The fourth tooth from the middle in the lower jaw is especially big.

▼ Alligators and caimans have teeth that are more or less the same size all along their jaws. They may show their teeth when their mouths are closed.

▲ ▼ The gavial and its cousin, the false gavial, have very long narrow snouts, with slender, pointed teeth that are ideal for catching fish. When these animals close their mouths, their needlelike teeth hardly show at all.

A Nile crocodile swimming in the Grumeti River in Tanzania. The crocodile has to work hard in the strong current and holds its head well above the water.

Where Crocodiles Live

The Nile crocodile lives beside water in hot parts of lowland Africa. Warm weather is important to the crocodile, because it is a cold-blooded animal. If its body temperature falls below about 77° F (25° C), it becomes very sluggish. If it becomes too hot, the crocodile simply slides into the water to cool off or presses its body into cool mud.

The crocodile needs water, not just to drink, but also to hide and to hunt in. The best home for a crocodile is a slow-flowing river or a lake with sandy banks. These places provide good nesting areas in the breeding season.

The crocodile is a powerful swimmer, moving its strong, oarlike tail from side to side. It can push itself through the water at tremendous speed. It uses its legs for steering. Crocodiles can swim in rough water, but they prefer not to. Fast-flowing water makes it impossible for a crocodile to disguise itself and drift down on to prey.

A young crocodile can stay underwater for at least 45 minutes without taking a breath. A big, old crocodile can probably stay submerged for more than two hours.

▼ Two Nile crocodiles basking on a sandbank. They are warmed by the sun, but press their bodies into the cool sand and keep their mouths open so that moisture evaporates. These actions prevent them from becoming too hot.

A Crocodile Is Born

About a month after mating, a female Nile crocodile is ready to lay her eggs. During this time she looks for a suitable nest site in sandy soil on the banks of a river or lake. The nests are usually well separated, but if there are many crocodiles, they may nest close to each other.

▼ A Nile crocodile guarding her nest in the Okavango Delta in Botswana

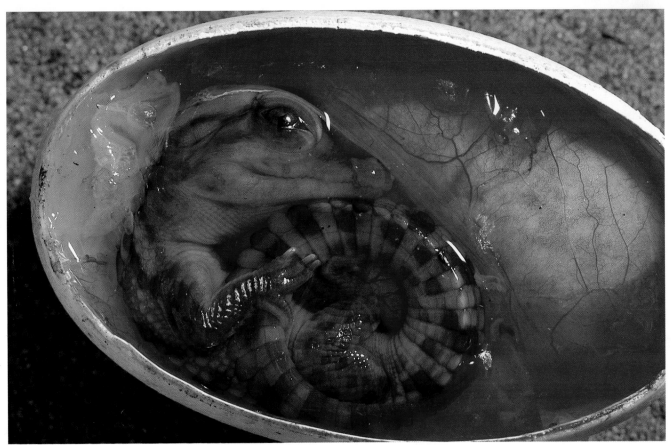

▲ Scientists have cut into this crocodile's egg several weeks after it was laid. You can see the developing baby crocodile, or embryo, curled up beside the yolk, which is its food.

The nest may be over 328 ft. (100 m) from the water's edge, where it will be safe from flooding. It must have some shade, but not too much. With her hind feet, the female makes a bucket-shaped hole over 24 in. (60 cm) deep, into which she lays her eggs. She then covers the nest with soil.

When a female Nile crocodile has finished laying her eggs, she remains near the nest, often lying right across it. Sometimes the male stays nearby, too. But since a large male may mate with several females, he cannot guard all their nests at once.

Incubation

During the incubation period, which lasts for up to three months, the eggs are warmed by the heat of the soil. During this time the female does not normally leave the nest. She goes without food while she keeps watch over her eggs.

There are many animals that are ready to risk their lives to get at the big, nutritious eggs. Perhaps the worst enemies are monitor lizards. These large, flesh-eating reptiles dig out any unprotected nest with their long, sharp claws. Other enemies include mammals such as hyenas, wild dogs, and mongooses, and birds such as storks. The presence of the mother lying nearby is usually enough to deter these animals from raiding the nest.

▲ Monitor lizards are, in many places, the worst enemies of crocodiles and their eggs. Here, in the Serengeti National Park, two lizards have found an unguarded nest and are feasting on crocodile eggs.

A yellow-billed stork standing near a large crocodile. If a female crocodile leaves her nest, storks may try to take the eggs or the young when they first hatch.

At the time the eggs are laid, the sex of the young crocodiles inside the eggs is not certain. Whether males or females hatch depends on how warm it is inside the nest during the first three weeks of incubation. If the temperature is below about 89.6° F (32° C), more female babies will be born than males. If the temperature is higher, there will be more males.

Hatching

When the baby crocodiles are ready to hatch, they call to their mother from inside the eggs. When she hears them croaking, the female opens the nest, sometimes by digging with her front paws and sometimes by wiggling to push the sand away. If she does not do this, the young will not be able to escape, because the surface of the nest has become so hard. In fact a person would need a hammer and chisel to chip it open.

▼ A mother Nile crocodile frees her eggs from the covering of sandy soil, so that her young can hatch easily. She may even break some of the shells using her huge jaws more gently than at any other time.

▲ Some young crocodiles have to cut their own way out of the shell. They use the egg tooth on the tip of their snout. A fly has found a place to perch on the tip of this partly hatched crocodile's nose.

BREAKING OUT

A young crocodile can crack its eggshell without the help of its mother. On the very tip of a baby crocodile's snout is a tiny, sharp, wartlike lump formed from thickened skin. This is called the egg tooth. The baby crocodile swings its head from side to side inside the egg and the egg tooth cuts through the shell. The egg tooth falls off soon after the young crocodiles have hatched.

The young crocodiles struggle to free themselves from the eggs. Often their mother helps them by taking the eggs into her huge mouth and cracking the shells with her teeth. She does this very gently, so that her babies are not harmed.

▲ A mother crocodile carrying her newly hatched young in her mouth

To the Water

A newborn Nile crocodile is about 10 in. (25 cm) long. It looks fat because its belly still contains a good deal of egg yolk. The egg yolk will provide it with food for the first few months of its life.

When her family is free of the eggs, the mother crocodile must escort them to water. She may carry some of them in her mouth, but the others will walk to the water's edge, staying close to her. Predators such as storks and mongooses may try to grab a quick meal, but usually most of the family survives.

▼ Newly hatched crocodiles stay close to their mothers for several months. This baby, photographed on the Nile River in Uganda, is between 6 and 8 weeks old. It is resting on its mother's foot.

Growing Up

Once in the water, the baby crocodiles cluster together in groups called pods. They have many enemies, including big wading birds, large fish, and terrapins. Their mother stays close and warns them by making little waves in the water if she senses danger. If the young call to her, she rushes to protect them. Other nearby crocodiles may also come to help. Often baby crocodiles ride on their mother's back in the water. They stick close to her when she goes ashore to bask.

▲ A mother crocodile watches some of her family as they venture out of the Nile River in Uganda. While they are this small, she will be very aggressive to any possible enemies.

The mother does not feed her babies. For up to six months, the remains of egg yolk inside their bodies helps to nourish the young crocodiles. Fortunately, at the time that the eggs hatch, insects are usually plentiful. These are the young crocodiles' first real food.

In the dry season, the water level falls, and food may become scarce. Young crocodiles are then in danger of being eaten by the adults that protected them just a short time ago.

▼ This young hatchling may be having its very first meal—a red dragonfly that it has snatched from its perch.

Getting Bigger

By the time that it is two years old, a Nile crocodile is about 3 ft. (1 m) long. This is four times as long as when it was born. Soon, it will begin to grow more slowly. Unlike most animals, which stop growing at a certain age, crocodiles keep growing throughout their whole lives.

In its first two years, a crocodile will have lost many of its brothers and sisters to predators such as hornbills, large lizards, hyenas, and otters. It is also becoming wary of older, aggressive crocodiles. It stays in a group with the other young crocodiles, keeping its distance from its elders.

▲ A survivor from a brood that hatched over a year ago. This young crocodile basks on a piece of fallen tree, from where it can escape quickly into the water.

► Seen from below as it swims, the Nile crocodile shows its powerful, oarlike tail and its webbed hind feet.

At this time, the young crocodile begins to change its lifestyle. It leaves the shallow water that has been its home up to now, and moves into deeper water.

Although it could swim as soon as it hatched, the young crocodile now begins to really use its swimming skills. It can float just below the surface of the water, or drive forward with a powerful swish of its oarlike tail to surprise prey. As the crocodile swims, its legs are tucked by its sides, except when they are needed for steering or stopping.

Finding Food

As they move into deeper water, the young crocodiles begin to change their diet. Their food includes many fish, and they may grab the birds that had previously hunted them when they were babies. They may also prey on rats or porcupines that drink at the water's edge. But they do not yet attack really large mammals.

Young crocodiles also look for stones to swallow, sometimes traveling long distances to find them. The stones lodge in the front part of the stomach and probably help to break up food. They are needed because the crocodile's sharp teeth are only good for holding prey, not for chewing food. The stones also act like a ship's ballast, evening up the weight distribution in the young crocodile's body. Then it can float flat in the water, rather than at an angle.

▼ Crocodiles seem to spend much of their lives resting. This one has retreated into the water, perhaps because of the heat. It can stay like this, without taking a breath, for about an hour.

▲ This crocodile is resting by the side of a river in Botswana. The sun is pouring down on it, but it is losing heat from its body by lying with its jaws open.

Temperature Control

Crocodiles spend a good deal of their time out of water, lying in the sun. This warms their bodies to a temperature that enables them to be active. But in Africa, the sun's rays can sometimes be too hot. So crocodiles often bask with their mouths open. This allows them to lose heat and stay cool.

Social Life

Crocodiles have a code of conduct that enables them to live together peacefully. The biggest and oldest crocodiles are the bosses of the group. The young animals keep out of their way, resting at the edge of the basking area and steering clear of them when they are in the water.

A crocodile can communicate in simple ways. It has scent glands on its jaw and under its tail. The smells they produce tell other crocodiles what the crocodile's rank is within the group.

▼ In order to survive, these young crocodiles must keep away from big old crocodiles that live in the same area.

24

▲ Crocodiles do not cooperate with others in most aspects of their lives. But an injured prey animal will attract a number of crocodiles, each hoping for a share of the meal.

The crocodile also uses its body to communicate. In water, a dominant crocodile uses head-slapping to declare its position and probably to warn lower-ranking crocodiles to stay away. The crocodile lies on the water's surface with its mouth open. Suddenly, it slams its jaws shut with a loud noise and a splash, which can be heard for long distances. Sometimes it thrashes its tail, creating noise and waves that scare off approaching youngsters.

An adult crocodile usually hunts for itself. But if one crocodile catches prey that is unusually large, others will come to share in the meal. A young crocodile would not dare to join in this shared meal. If it tried to, it would probably be attacked by its elders.

Adulthood

A crocodile doing a high walk as it leaves the water. Its body is held clear of the ground, almost like a mammal.

Crocodiles are called opportunist feeders, which means that they take almost any food they can, whenever it is available. Once they are adults, most of their kills are made in the water.

Crocodiles have surprisingly quick reactions. They are fast enough even to snatch birds such as herons or storks at the waterside. Mammals are also at risk. Crocodiles can throw antelope off balance with a single blow from their heads or a powerful swish of their tails.

A MEAL A WEEK

Nile crocodiles are highly efficient killers, but they do not need to feed often. If food is scarce, they can go for months without eating. On average, a big crocodile will kill about 50 times a year. This is slightly less than once a week.

How They Move

Crocodiles usually crawl slowly on land, but they can, if frightened, go much faster. They do this by using what is called a belly run. This involves sliding over sloping, muddy ground, by using their feet. When making overland journeys and when moving at high speed for short distances, they "high walk." The legs are tucked under the body, and the crocodile lopes along, almost like a cat.

Young crocodiles can also gallop. Over short distances they can bound along at speeds of up to 7.5 miles per hour (12 kph).

▶ Crocodiles sometimes leap vertically from the water, usually in an attempt to catch a bird.

Hunting in Water

In many lakes and rivers, Nile crocodiles feed mainly on fish. In others, their prey are large mammals, such as zebras, buffalo, impalas, and wildebeests. The animals come to the water to drink, but do not see the crocodile lurking a few feet away. Only the top of its head shows, looking like a piece of floating wood.

When the animal is bending down quenching its thirst, the crocodile shoots forward and grabs it by the nose. The struggle is not an even one. On the slippery riverbank, the prey is soon dragged under the water, where it is held and drowned. Even if it breaks free, the crocodile is likely to grab it again and inflict terrible wounds with its sharp teeth. Escape is very rare.

▼ A hunting crocodile probably looks like a floating log to most animals. A prey animal might realize the danger if it could see the crocodile's bright eyes. But many do not until it is too late and the crocodile's jaws close on them.

▲ Migrating
wildebeests cross the
Grumeti River in the
Serengeti. Every year
crocodiles lie in wait
at the traditional
crossing places and
ambush the wildebeest
as they enter the
water.

One problem that faces all crocodiles is how to
eat large prey. Crocodile teeth are perfect for
holding things, but useless for biting chunks out
of them. A crocodile with a large kill seizes a limb
or the head and then spins around in the water.
Eventually it tears the flesh from the body.

Other crocodiles from the group may be attracted
to the scene of the kill. Working together, they
balance each other's weight so that even the
largest of prey is torn apart easily.

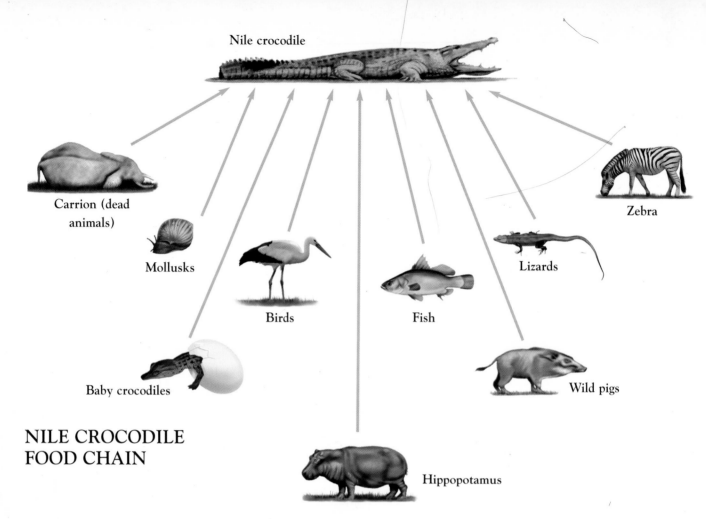

Nile crocodile

Carrion (dead animals)

Mollusks

Birds

Fish

Lizards

Zebra

Baby crocodiles

Wild pigs

NILE CROCODILE FOOD CHAIN

Hippopotamus

Crocodiles and Other Animals

Almost all a Nile crocodile's animal neighbors are possible sources of food. Throughout its life, a crocodile feeds on a large variety of creatures. It starts with insects when it is very young and moves on to snails, freshwater crabs, fish, terrapins, lizards, rodents, and mammals.

The risk to crocodiles from their neighbors is very small, because most of the animals they attack have no real defense. However, one Nile crocodile was attacked and killed by a pride of lions when it tried to steal their food. Such incidents are rare.

▲ The crocodile is at the top of its food chain. It eats a wide variety of other creatures.

The most common large enemy of the Nile crocodile is the hippopotamus. During the breeding season, male hippos are extremely short-tempered and aggressive. Also, a female hippo whose calf is threatened by a crocodile will turn on the aggressor. There are many accounts of crocodiles that were injured or even killed by the huge teeth of an angry hippopotamus.

▼ A spur-winged plover. These birds help crocodiles by eating parasites inside their mouths.

TEETH-CLEANING BIRDS

Certain birds, such as spur-winged plovers, will use a basking crocodile as a feeding table. The birds creep between the crocodile's open jaws to pick scraps of meat from its teeth. The crocodile puts up with the birds' attention, probably because they also remove uncomfortable, leechlike parasites from the crocodiles' mouths.

Finding a Mate

Nile crocodiles usually mate for the first time between the ages of twelve and fifteen. By this time the males are about 10 ft. (3 m) and the females nearly 8 ft. (2.5 m).

The breeding season of the Nile crocodile varies. In South Africa, breeding occurs in the summer, between September and December. Farther north, where temperatures vary little throughout the year, breeding mostly occurs in the dry season. This way the young hatch as the rains are about to start and water in rivers and lakes begins to rise.

▼ Two male crocodiles challenge each other for the right to mate. They may fight, but probably neither will be seriously hurt.

▲ The winning male will court suitable females in his territory. He touches their snouts with his, and nudges their necks, often for several hours, before they finally mate.

At the start of the breeding season, males become aggressive, so large males may fight each other. Sometimes they will attack other creatures, such as hippos or even small boats, which they probably mistake for rivals.

Crocodiles are noisy during courtship. The males roar and can sound like lions or distant thunder. They also make a noise like a barking cough. The females reply with a growling roar. The male rears out of the water with gaping jaws to impress a potential female mate. He later caresses the female's head with his own before mating with her. After mating, the pair separate and seem completely uninterested in each other.

Life Span

It is difficult to tell a crocodile's age, but we do know that the biggest crocodiles are also the oldest. This is because crocodiles continue to grow throughout their lives. They grow fastest for the first seven years, adding about 11 in. (28 cm) to their length each year. After this, they continue to grow, but more slowly. They increase in size by only 2 in. (4 cm) per year.

A crocodile 18 ft. (5.5 m) long may be as much as a hundred years old. Under a microscope, patterns of growth can be seen on a crocodile's osteoderms. These growth patterns can be used to calculate the crocodile's age. It has been suggested that some Nile crocodiles may live until they are about 200 years old.

◀ A very big crocodile, like this one, is bound to be very old, probably over 100 years. Some people think that it may be even older, but it is difficult to be certain.

A Nile crocodile has few natural enemies. Occasionally, a mother elephant will kill a crocodile that tries to attack its baby. She tramples the crocodile, killing it with her great weight. Or she may even throw its dead body up into a tree.

Parasites and disease may kill some crocodiles, as may changes to their habitat that affect the supply of food and water. Some male crocodiles may die after being injured during fights with rival males during the breeding season.

▲ Elephants and crocodiles normally ignore each other, but if a baby elephant strays from its mother, it may be attacked. There are many cases known of elephants killing crocodiles in such circumstances.

Crocodiles and People

For much of history, crocodiles in Africa were respected as special animals. In many societies, people did not hunt crocodiles because they believed they were their tribal ancestors. Individual crocodiles were sometimes worshiped and fed humans. In other areas, people accused of crimes were forced to swim across crocodile-infested rivers. If they were not attacked, they were declared innocent.

Crocodiles were thought to be able to work powerful magic. Potions containing crocodile fat were sometimes used to guard against bad luck, including being struck by lightning. Wearing a crocodile's tooth or claw was also believed to protect against attacks from crocodiles.

▼ The strength of a crocodile's jaws made people of the past believe that crocodiles must be animals with special magic powers.

▶ Ancient Egyptians, who lived nearly 4,000 years ago, showed their god Sebek in carvings, like this one, and paintings. He had the body of a man and the head of a crocodile.

CROCODILE GOD

The ancient Egyptians worshiped a crocodile-headed god called Sebek. The center of his worship was at a town called Crocodilopolis. At shrines to Sebek, crocodiles were decorated with gold ornaments. They were fed meat, bread, milk, and honey brought as gifts by travelers.

Perhaps these beliefs came about because people were afraid of crocodiles and had little defense against them. Crocodiles are one of the few animals that do not seem to dislike human flesh. Some experts suggest that about 300 people are still killed each year by Nile crocodiles.

Threats

Over time, people began to respect crocodiles less and hunt them more. In the last one hundred years, the number of Nile crocodiles has fallen dramatically. In some places, such as South Africa, people tried to eliminate crocodiles entirely, because they were considered to be dangerous pests. Hunters were given bounties for killing them.

Even more Nile crocodiles were killed when people realized that crocodile skins could be used to make high quality leather goods. Between 1950 and 1980, at least three million Nile crocodiles were killed.

▼ These African animal products are made from endangered species, including crocodiles and elephants. They were imported illegally into the United States, where they were discovered and taken.

Another threat facing Nile crocodiles are the changes to their habitat caused by human activity. For example, draining a swamp for use as farmland may make the area too dry for the Nile crocodiles to survive. And taking vast amounts of water from lakes to irrigate farmland can make the lake water too salty for the crocodiles to live in. Increased fishing on some lakes is resulting in more and more crocodiles getting trapped and drowned in fishing nets.

▲ A dead crocodile lies beside a drying riverbed. Changes in the environment have meant that many places in Africa are no longer suitable for crocodiles to survive in.

Protecting Crocodiles

By the 1950s, Nile crocodiles were rare in many places where they were once common. Every animal has a complex web of relationships with other animals. It was found that when crocodiles disappeared from an area, other animals suffered as well. For example, the numbers of fish fell in some places, because the crocodiles were no longer eating the creatures that preyed on the fish.

In 1955, Kenya banned hunting Nile crocodiles for their skins, although it was many years before other countries did the same. Zambia, for example, did not ban hunting them until 1987. Even so, the decline in crocodile numbers has slowed down.

▲ Crocodile protection makes the killing of most wild crocodiles illegal. This picture shows part of a haul of about 1,300 poached crocodile skins, which are about to be destroyed. This means that neither the poachers nor anybody else can make a profit from killing wild crocodiles.

The Convention on International Trade in Endangered Species (CITES) was set up in 1973. CITES makes it illegal to buy and sell wild animals from rare species, including the Nile crocodile. Most African states have now signed the convention. There is still some illegal poaching and trading, which African governments are trying to stop.

In a few places, human activities have actually helped Nile crocodiles. After the building of the Aswan Dam on the Nile River, for example, crocodiles returned to places where they had not been seen for many years. The dam has made the river flow more evenly, which suits the crocodiles.

▼ Young crocodiles, often crudely stuffed, are sometimes illegally offered as tourist souvenirs.

Crocodile Farming

Crocodile farms have been set up in some African countries to satisfy the demand for crocodile leather and to help wild Nile crocodiles at the same time.

In the past, young crocodiles were collected from the wild and reared in captivity, but they did not always settle well into their new homes. Now eggs are collected instead. The eggs are usually taken shortly before they are due to hatch. The young crocodiles have plenty of food and grow fast on the farm. They are killed when they are two years old, producing good quality skins and meat.

▼ Young crocodiles on a crocodile farm in Tanzania. Raising them in this way has brought a new industry to some parts of Africa. It has also protected wild populations of Nile crocodiles. The worker takes care to handle his sharp-toothed stock at a safe distance!

▲ Well-fed and cared-for young crocodiles bask near their pools in a crocodile farm in Namibia. They grow quickly, and in time their legally produced leather will help to bring wealth to the country.

Farmed crocodile skins are given CITES tags, which identify them, so they can be used legally to make leather goods throughout the world. Farming Nile crocodiles has already brought wealth and food to some areas of Africa.

You can find out more about crocodiles and some of the organizations working to help them by using the information on page 47.

Crocodile Life Cycle

 **1** The female lays her eggs in a nest near water. She stays by the nest to guard it against predators.

 **2** When the eggs are ready to hatch, the mother crocodile digs them out of the nest. She takes the newly hatched crocodiles to a nearby lake or river, where they feed on insects.

 **3** As they grow, the baby crocodiles leave their mother and move into deeper water. Their food now includes fish, crabs, water snails, birds, and rodents. They swallow stones to help their digestion and balance in the water.

 **4** When they are seven or eight years old, the young crocodiles join the main group of adults. Young crocodiles are wary of the biggest oldest animals, which might attack them.

 **5** Between the ages of twelve and fifteen, a crocodile will breed for the first time. It is now big enough to prey on medium-sized mammals, such as antelope, but fish probably make up most of its diet.

 **6** A really old crocodile can live for more than one hundred years and grow to more than 16 ft. (5 m) long. It dominates the group in which it lives and can overcome large prey, such as buffalo and young giraffes.

Glossary

Ballast Heavy material used to keep a ship steady in the water.

Cold-blooded An animal with a body temperature that varies with the warmth of its surroundings.

Dominant The lead animal in a group. It is usually the strongest.

Estuary A water passage where the tide meets a river current.

Incubation The period between when an egg is laid and when it hatches, during which it must be kept warm.

Mammals A group of warm-blooded animals that feed their young on milk produced by mammary glands. Mammals include humans, lions, and hippos.

Osteoderms Bony scales that crocodiles and some other animals have set into their skin. They make an effective armor.

Parasites Animals that live and feed on or in the bodies of other animals.

Poaching Hunting and killing animals illegally.

Pod A group of animals; for example, young crocodiles or whales.

Predator A animal that kills and eats other animals.

Prey An animal that is hunted and eaten by predators.

Scent glands Parts of an animal's body that produce smelly liquids called scents.

Terrapin A type of turtle that lives in water.

Warm-blooded An animal that has a constant body temperature, whether the surroundings are hot or cold. They need more food than cold-blooded animals.

Further Information

Organizations to Contact

World Wildlife Fund
1250 Twenty-Fourth Street, N.W.
P.O. Box 97180
Washington, DC 20077-7180
1-800-CALL-WWF
www.worldwildlife.org

CITES Secretariat
15 Chemin des Anemones
1219 Chatelaine-Geneva, Switzerland
(4122) 917 8139/40
www.cites.org

Websites

The Gator Hole
home.cfl.rr.com/gatorhole

Crocodilians Natural History &
Conservation
www.crocodilian.com

The Discovery Channel
www.discovery.com

Books to Read

Dudley, Karen. *Alligators & Crocodiles.*
Raintree Steck-Vaughn, 1998.

Petty, Kate. *Crocodiles Yawn to Keep Cool.*
Copper Beech Books, 1998.

Simon, Seymour. *Crocodiles & Alligators.*
HarperCollins, 1999.

Stone, Lynn M. *Alligators and Crocodiles.*
Children's Press, 1998.

Wallace, Karen. *Imagine You Are a Crocodile.*
Henry Holt & Company, 1997.

Woodward, John. *Crocodiles & Alligators.*
Marshall Cavendish, 1998.

Index

All the numbers in **bold** refer to photographs or illustrations.

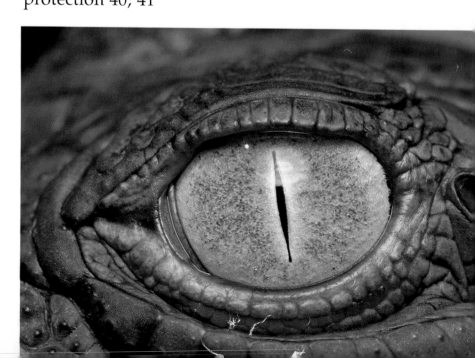